Tuning In

Using the teaching notes, start by reading pages 2 and 3 together as a group, then give each child a section to read. When they have read the section, ask them to write down a word or two to remind them of new things they have learnt. Use the teaching notes to support the children as they read. Finish the lesson by drawing the group back together and asking the children what facts they have learnt.

The front cover

Let's look at the title together. What do you think this book will tell us about rivers?

Do you know the names of any rivers?

What do you think rivers can be used for?

The back cover

What does the blurb tell us?

What will this book be about?

Using the River

Claire Llewellyn

Contents

Scan the contents list and find which page is about 'Water Power'.

Skim down the page again and find the page that tells us how water is stored.

Where is the glossary?

LESSON 1

Read pages 2 and 3

Purpose: to learn about different kinds of rivers.

Pause at page 3

(Ask the children to skim through the introduction to find out how rivers might be used.)

What three things have we learnt about how rivers might be used? (*making electricity, transporting people and goods, providing food*)

What other facts have we learnt about rivers?

Read pages 4 and 5

Purpose: to learn how a river is formed and how it changes.

Pause at page 5

Where do most rivers start and where are they going?

What happens to the snow and the rain?

Look at the photograph on page 5. Can you see the river and the sea?

When does the river move fast?

When does it move more slowly?

Introduction

Think of a river. It could be a rushing torrent, a busy waterway or a quiet country stream.

Rivers can be used in all sorts of ways. Some rivers are used to make **electricity**. Some are used to transport people and their goods.

Rivers can also provide food and water to many kinds of living things.

Some rivers flow for thousands of miles.

They pass through deep gorges, wide valleys and dry, empty fields. They flow past cities, towns and farms.

The Changing River

A river is water that is on its way to the sea.

The journey starts high on mountains and hills. The heavy rainfall and melting snow trickle down the mountain and join up to form tiny streams.

The streams flow together and form a river. The young river races downhill.

When the river reaches flat land, it changes again. It flows more slowly. It is older, wider and deeper now. It winds its way gently to the sea.

READ

Read pages 6 and 7

Purpose: to find out why plants like to grow on the sides of rivers,

to use the glossary to understand technical terms ('nutrients').

Pause at page 7

Why is the river a good place for plants to grow?

What does the soil contain near the river's edge?

Who can tell me what nutrients are? How can we find out? (*glossary*) How do we know? (*because the word's in bold*) How do we know where to find the glossary? (Help the children look it up on the contents page.)

What happens to the seeds of the trees when they fall into the water?

Tricky word (page 6):
The word 'nutrients' may be beyond the children's word recognition skills. Tell this word to the children.

Plants Use Rivers

A river is a good place for plants to grow. The water is full of **nutrients**. The muddy riverbank has rich soil because it contains the rotting remains of plants.

▲ Some plants grow in deep water. They have stems that grow up from the river floor.

▲ Other plants stay in shallow water, in the soggy ground near the bank.

Trees along the riverbank drop their seeds in the water below. The river carries the seeds to another place where new trees can grow. ▼

6

7

Read pages 8 and 9

Purpose: to find out which different animals use the river,

to find two facts about living in and near a river.

Pause at page 9

Why do some animals live near fast flowing streams?

What is a baby swan called? (*cygnet*)

What does the arrow mean beside the first caption?

What two facts have you learnt about animals that live in and near the river?

Read pages 10 and 11

Purpose: to find 5 things that people need water for;

to practise getting information from photographs.

Pause at page 11

What 5 things do people need water for?

What are the people doing in the photograph on page 11?

What makes you think this photograph was not taken in Britain?

*Please turn to page 15 for **Revisit and Respond** activities.*

Animals Use Rivers

A river makes a very good habitat for all kinds of animals. Snails, insects, fish, frogs, voles, otters and birds all live in or near rivers.

Some animals make their homes in fast-flowing streams where the water is cold and clean. But most animals live in a quieter part of the river where the water is deep and slow.

Swans raise their ▶ young by the river.

8

◀ Small creatures live in and near the river.

▲ Oxygen in the river water allows fish to breathe.

▲ Rivers are good places to build a home.

9

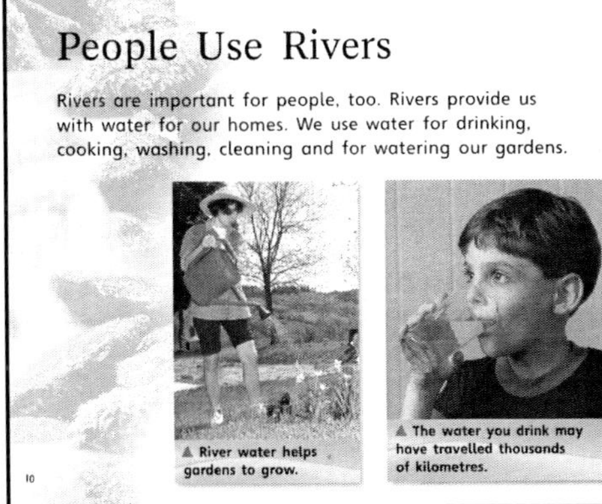

People Use Rivers

Rivers are important for people, too. Rivers provide us with water for our homes. We use water for drinking, cooking, washing, cleaning and for watering our gardens.

▲ River water helps gardens to grow.

▲ The water you drink may have travelled thousands of kilometres.

10

▲ Some rivers are sacred. In this picture people are praying and bathing in the holy water of the River Ganges.

Some people have no running water in their homes. Rivers can supply these people with most of their water needs.

11

Tricky word (page 11):

The word 'Ganges' may be beyond the children's word recognition skills. Tell this word to the children.

LESSON 2

Read pages 12 and 13

Purpose: to find out two ways in which water reaches the crop,

to use the glossary to find the meaning of the technical terms 'channels' and 'irrigation'.

Pause at page 13

Which two ways do farmers get water to their crops?

What would happen if the crops were not irrigated?

Read pages 14 and 15

Purpose: to find out why people build dams and reservoirs,

to scan the page to find the word 'dam'.

Pause at page 15

What may happen to rivers in the summer?

Why do people build dams?

What is the water in reservoirs used for?

Where would you find an explanation for the word 'dam'?

Tricky words (page 14):

The words 'reservoir' and 'Itaipu' may be beyond the children's word recognition skills. Tell these words to the children.

READ

Read pages 16 and 17

Purpose: to find out how water power is used,

to use the glossary to understand the technical terms 'turbines' and 'generator'.

Pause at page 17

What is the water power used for?

How does it help to make electricity?

READ

Read pages 18 and 19

Purpose: to find out what rivers have in common with roads,

to use the glossary to find the meaning of the technical terms 'cargo' and 'barges'.

Pause at page 19

Why are the rivers described as roads?

What are the largest rivers like?

What kinds of boats use the rivers for transporting goods?

Water Power

Power stations are often built next to dams. Inside the power station, electricity is made by directing the flow of water into pipes. The water in the pipes turns the turbines which make electricity.

This dam has opened its gates.

▲ The power of the water turns special wheels called **turbines**. The turbines create energy that is changed into electricity by a **generator**.

16

17

Roads of Water

Rivers are like roads. They make good travel routes through forests, mountains and hills. Rivers are useful for transporting goods. Boats deliver materials to the factories and then collect the goods when they are made.

▲ Some cargo ships head for the open sea as others make their way into port.

18

▲ Tugboats push barges that are loaded with goods.

The world's largest rivers are like main roads. Instead of lorries, heavy **barges** are used to transport goods.

19

Tricky word (page 17):

The word 'generator' may be beyond the children's word recognition skills. Help them to break this word down into four syllables, before blending the whole word together.

Read pages 20 and 21

Purpose: to find out why rivers flood.

Pause at page 21

Why do rivers flood?

Why is this dangerous?

What can we learn from the captions about the ways people try to prevent flooding?

Read pages 22 and 23

Purpose: to find out the different ways people enjoy using the rivers.

Pause at page 23

Why do people visit rivers?

What do people like doing on the river?

Why should we look after our rivers?

Floods

People cannot always control rivers. Sometimes they can be dangerous. Heavy rain and melting snow can make the water level rise suddenly. When there is too much water in the river, the river will flood.

A big flood can destroy houses and crops, and can threaten the lives of people and animals.

20

▲ People who live near rivers often try and stop floods by raising the riverbanks.

▲ Sometimes new river channels are built in order to hold extra flood-water.

21

Enjoying the River

Most of the time, rivers are beautiful places. People visit them to rest, relax and have fun.

Some people like to walk along the riverbank. Others like to fish.

Many people enjoy water sports on the river. They can paddle a canoe over white-water **rapids** or cruise along gently downstream.

22

Rivers are used in many different ways by people, plants and animals.

And because they are so important to all living things, we need to look after and care for all of our rivers.

23

READ

Read page 24

Purpose: to practise using a glossary and an index.

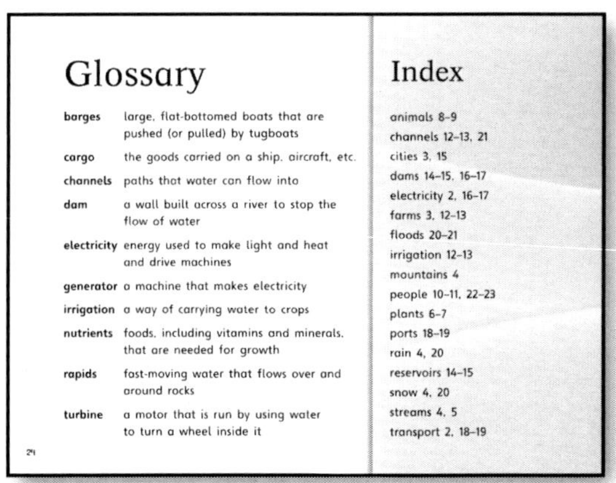

Glossary

barges	large, flat-bottomed boats that are pushed (or pulled) by tugboats
cargo	the goods carried on a ship, aircraft, etc.
channels	paths that water can flow into
dam	a wall built across a river to stop the flow of water
electricity	energy used to make light and heat and drive machines
generator	a machine that makes electricity
irrigation	a way of carrying water to crops
nutrients	foods, including vitamins and minerals, that are needed for growth
rapids	fast-moving water that flows over and around rocks
turbine	a motor that is run by using water to turn a wheel inside it

24

Index

EXPLORE

Pause at page 24

How does a glossary help us?

Who can find the definition of 'rapids'?

What do you notice about the definitions? (*not full sentences, no capital letters, very brief*)

Why do you think an index is in alphabetical order?

Why are several pages listed beside the word 'people'?

Where will you find out about reservoirs?

After Reading

Revisit and Respond

Lesson 1

- What facts have you learnt about how rivers are formed and where they go to?
- How did the headings help you to find out what the book was going to be about?
- Look at the headings on pages 4, 6, and 8. Change these headings into questions. (*e.g. How do rivers change?*)
- Scan the book for examples to use in a wall display of words about water.

Lesson 2

- Look at pages 12, 20 and 22. Each of these pages has more than one paragraph. Think of a heading for each paragraph.
- What do you know now that you did not know before reading this book?
- Look at the glossary on page 24. Ask individual children to turn different entries into full sentences (*Barges are flat-bottomed. A dam is a wall. etc*)
- Brainstorm suitable adjectives and list them under the headings 'Rushing Torrent' and 'Slow Stream'.

Follow-up

Independent Group Activity Work

The book is accompanied by two photocopy masters, one with a reading focus and one with a writing focus, which support the teaching objectives of this book.

The photocopy masters can be found in the *Planning and Assessment Guide.*

PCM NF2.1 *(reading)*

PCM NF2.2 *(writing)*

You may also like to invite the children to read the text again during their independent reading (either at school or at home).

Writing

Guided writing: Discuss with the group the journey a river makes from source to sea. Help the children to draw and label a diagram showing what happens to the river on this journey.

Extended writing: Ask the children to choose a section from the book and make notes on the information it contains.

Assessment Points

Assess that the children have learnt the main teaching points of the book by checking that they can:

- explain organisational features of texts, including looking up information in an index and a glossary, alphabetical order and captions.